KID OCEANOGRAPHER

DISCOVER AMAZING SPECIES, MARINE ECOSYSTEMS & UNDERWATER MARVELS

APPLESAUCE PRESS

EXPLORE THE MYSTERIES
OF THE OCEAN DEEP

TABLE OF CONTENTS

INTRODUCTION

Water, water, everywhere! Oceans cover about 70% of the planet—that's two-thirds of Earth! And oceans contain more than 96% of Earth's water. Oceanographers explore and study it all, from the water to the waves to the wildlife. Millions of plants and animals call the ocean home. We don't even know how many animal species live there, because the ocean is so huge and deep we haven't been able to explore it all—yet.

Learning about oceans is more important than ever. Climate change, pollution, and human activity can make the water dirtier and warmer, which makes it harder for animals to live there comfortably. Oceanographers want to protect the plants and animals living in the ocean, so they study how the water movement and temperature change over time. The more they understand about what's changing, the better they can help protect ocean habitats. Scientists aren't the only ones responsible for keeping our oceans safe. Knowledge is power, and everyone can take steps to learn more about the ocean.

Let's dive in!

OCEANOGRAPHY 101

Oceanography is exactly what it sounds like—it's the study of the ocean. Oceanographers study everything in and around the ocean. That includes the seafloor, the water, the waves, the shore, the plants, and the animals. They also study the impact that humans have on ocean life. Oceanographers research, run experiments, and collect data, but the biggest part of their job is fieldwork. That means they spend most of their time working in, on, or near the water to study the ocean firsthand. Lots of oceanographers will learn to boat or scuba dive so that they can get up close and personal with the ocean.

So how does someone become an oceanographer? You need a lot of scientific training, especially in earth sciences. In college, studying chemistry, physics, biology, geology, and/or marine biology is a great starting point to get into oceanography. Many oceanographers will go on to get a master's degree or doctorate degree in one of the four branches of oceanography: biological, physical, geological, and chemical oceanography.

Some questions that oceanographers are asking right now include: How much microplastic—bits of plastic that have gotten into the environment and which have been broken down until they are very tiny—have found their way into the ocean? How do animals feed themselves in the deepest depths of the ocean, where there is no sunlight? Can we predict how much rain will fall further into the future? And so many more!

As you might expect, oceanographers use a lot of different tools to look into questions like these. Oceanographers' tools can be very simple, like the common net, used to catch animals near the water's surface, and the bucket, used to collect samples of surface water. But they can also be very complex, like the 60-year-old submersible vehicle known as Alvin, which can transport three people to a depth of over 14,000 feet (4,270 meters)—2.8 miles (4.5 kilometers) down!

Have you ever been to the beach and done some "oceanographing" yourself? What kinds of things were you curious about?

Biological oceanographers study all of the life-forms in the ocean. They learn about all of the plants and animals in different environments, study how they grow and change, and watch how they interact with one another.

Chemical oceanographers study the chemicals that make up seawater. They look at how water is different depending on where it is on the planet, and they learn what causes the chemicals in the water to change. They also study how different chemicals in the water affect marine life.

Geological oceanographers study the ocean floor and the different geographic features it has, including mountains, valleys, canyons, basins, and even volcanoes. They research the movement of tectonic plates (see page 29) and watch how the ocean floor changes over time.

Physical oceanographers study the movement of the water. They research waves, tides, and currents, and learn about how the weather and climate change the movement of the water. They also study coastal erosion and the ways light and sound move through water.

WHO'S WHO

Let's meet ten influential oceanographers.

Jacques Cousteau was best known for co-inventing the Aqua-Lung, which led to the creation of modern scuba (self-contained underwater breathing apparatus) gear. He used the equipment to film underwater. He wrote books about his undersea explorations and made award-winning documentaries with the underwater footage.

Sylvia Earle is an oceanographer who researched marine algae. She wrote books and made documentaries to raise awareness about the threat of overfishing and pollution to the ocean. In 1998, *Time* magazine named her its first Hero for the Planet. The same year, she became an Explorer-in-Residence for the National Geographic Society.

Kathryn Sullivan is both an oceanographer and an astronaut. Most people know her best for being the first woman to walk in space, but she also studied the ocean floor. When she left NASA, she became chief scientist at the National Oceanic and Atmospheric Administration (NOAA).

Matthew Fontaine Maury is considered to be one of the founders of oceanography. He studied the winds and currents and made charts of the Atlantic, Pacific, and Indian Oceans. In 1855 his book *The Physical Geography of the Sea* was the first major book on oceanography to ever be published.

Walter Munk was a leader in studying ocean currents. He researched surface waves, the effect of Earth's rotation on currents, and tides. He used acoustic measurements (waves of vibration and sound) and temperature measurements to understand the way sound travels in the ocean.

Sir John Murray was another founder in the field of oceanography, in the branch of biology. He was especially interested in coral reefs, and he was well-known for the samples he collected on his expeditions. Several animal species, including an octopus and a sea sponge, are named after him.

Robert S. Dietz was best known for his theory on seafloor spreading. It's an important theory in understanding plate tectonics (see page 29) and the way that the seafloor spreads out and changes over time.

Fridtjof Nansen was an explorer and Nobel Peace Prize winner who made many voyages, especially in the North Atlantic Ocean. He also helped to improve modern oceanographic equipment.

Robert Ballard is a pioneer in underwater archaeology (studying human history). He discovered several important shipwrecks, including the *Titanic* and the *Bismarck*. Many of his explorations were done by underwater rovers called submersibles (see page 20), which sent video feed of the wrecks back to Ballard and his team on a nearby ship.

Columbus O'Donnell Iselin was a director of the Woods Hole Oceanographic Institution in Massachusetts. He helped turn it into one of the largest institutions for oceanographic research.

OUR OCEANS

All of the oceans on Earth are connected, and they make up one large, continuous body of salt water called the World Ocean. The oceans don't really have boundaries the way that landmasses do, but for the sake of geography and mapmaking the oceans are named based on the continents around them. The World Ocean is most often divided into five major oceans.

Asia

ARCTIC OCEAN

The Arctic is the smallest of the oceans, and it extends up from Greenland and Iceland to the North Pole. It touches the top of North America, Siberia, and Scandinavia. This polar ocean is usually partially frozen, especially around the North Pole.

PACIFIC OCEAN

The Pacific is the largest and deepest ocean, but it shrinks a bit every year because of tectonic plate movement. It reaches between Australia, Asia, and the western coasts of North and South America, and it contains over 20,000 islands.

North America

SOUTHERN OCEAN

The Southern Ocean is the "newest" of the oceans. This section surrounds Antarctica and is the second-smallest of the oceans. It's the windiest ocean, and it is often partially covered in ice.

Australia

ARCTIC OCEAN

ATLANTIC OCEAN

The Atlantic is the second-largest ocean, reaching between the Americas and West Africa and Europe. This ocean is affected by tectonic plate movement, and it gets a little bit wider each year.

Europe

Africa

INDIAN OCEAN

The Indian Ocean is the third-largest ocean and the warmest of the oceans. It surrounds India, the Arabian Peninsula, and Southeast Asia and it reaches from East Africa to Western Australia. This tropical ocean has lots of coral reefs, but it's prone to tsunamis.

South America

THE "SEVEN" SEAS

Pirate movies and stories of old-time mariners will often talk about the "seven seas." This term was used before the oceans were called oceans, and the seven seas of olden days included the Arctic, North Atlantic, South Atlantic, Indian, North Pacific, South Pacific, and Southern (or Antarctic) Oceans. Nowadays, we call these larger areas of salt water *oceans*, and the term *sea* more generally refers to a smaller area of salt water. Seas are still connected to the larger World Ocean, but the area is usually partially enclosed by land. Sometimes, "seas" are gulfs or bays, and sometimes they're areas that have different currents than other nearby water. There are more than 50 seas in the world, but calling something a sea or an ocean is just a way to geographically divide the water.

OCEANS OVER TIME

Earth hasn't always looked the way it does today, and neither has its oceans. The continents and oceans have changed location over time because of plate tectonics (see page 29). Some pre-historic oceans would have been in areas of the globe that are land today. We know where these prehistoric oceans would have been because of fossil findings. Life in the ocean has existed for millions of years, and it has been there for a lot longer than humans. There are some species of ocean animals (like sea sponges, see page 69) that have always lived in the water. Their ancestors were in the ocean millions of years ago, and they are today, too. But some animal species started out on land and eventually made their way to the sea. Whales are one example of this. Prehistoric ancestors of whales had legs and would have spent some of their time on land. But as they spent more time in the water, the legs became unnecessary. Eventually, they evolved to have no legs at all.

DARK DEPTHS

The ocean gets colder and darker the further down you go. Cold water is heavier than warm water, so it sinks down to the deeper parts of the ocean. As for it getting darker, it's pretty simple: the sun can't reach that far. There aren't any natural light sources coming from the depths, so it gets darker as you get further away from the surface. The water above you adds a lot of pressure the further down you go. People can't survive in areas with too much pressure, and neither can most animals. Oceanographers group the depth of the ocean into different zones.

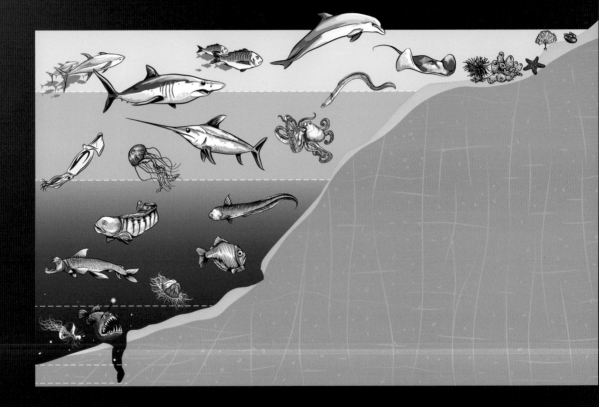

SUNLIGHT ZONE

TWILIGHT ZONE

MIDNIGHT ZONE

ABYSSAL ZONE
HADAL ZONE

SUNLIGHT ZONE

Oceanographers call the zone 0 to 660 feet (0 to 200 meters) below the surface the sunlight zone because this is the only zone where sunlight is visible. Sunlight makes photosynthesis possible, which is an important part of the aquatic food chain (see page 50). You'll find animals like fish, jellyfish, and dolphins in the sunlight zone. This zone is where most ocean animals spend their time, and it's also where you'll find environments like reefs and kelp forests (see page 44).

TWILIGHT ZONE

After the sunlight zone is the twilight zone, 660 to 3,300 feet (200 to 1,000 meters) below the surface. At this depth, there's barely any sunlight, and it's much harder for creatures living there to see. Some of the fish, jellyfish, and squids in this zone are bioluminescent. These animals have a unique chemical makeup that gives off some light. Bioluminescence helps animals to see one another, and some animals even use it to lure in prey.

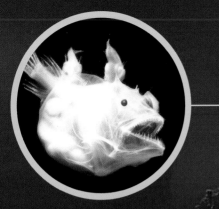

MIDNIGHT ZONE

Sunlight is completely gone in the midnight zone, which is 3,300 to 13,000 feet (1,000 to 4,000 meters) below the surface. Some animals, like whales, will briefly dive into this zone when they're hunting prey. But there are fish, octopuses, and squids that live in this zone. Some rely on bioluminescence. Others use special organs that help them sense movement, heat, and electrical fields. They might not be able to see, but they can feel other creatures around them!

ABYSSAL ZONE

As the ocean gets darker it also gets colder, and the abyssal zone 13,000 to 20,000 feet (1,000 to 6,000 meters) below the surface is extremely cold. A few creatures like sea sponges can survive in this zone, but for the most part you won't find any animals living in the big, flat stretches of ocean floor that make up the abyssal zone.

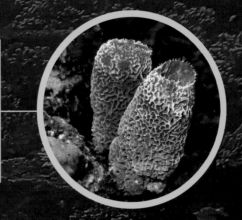

HADAL ZONE

The deepest part of the ocean is the hadal zone, 20,000 to 36,100 feet (6,000 to 11,000 meters) below the surface. The trenches in the hadal zone are pitch black, freezing cold, and under immense pressure. You'll find a few sea stars, worms, and some bacteria in this zone, but the conditions are too inhospitable for most living things. The Mariana Trench in the Pacific Ocean is the deepest part of the whole ocean. One section, called the Challenger Deep, is so deep that the whole of Mount Everest could fit in it completely underwater.

SEEN AND UNSEEN

More than 80% of the world's oceans is unexplored, so there's still a lot to learn. With so much left to discover, current ocean maps are far from complete. In fact, scientists have more detailed maps of the Moon, Mars, and Venus than they do of the ocean floor! If the ocean is so huge, how do scientists even know what's down there? Oceanographers have a few different ways of exploring the ocean. One is with their own eyes. A lot of oceanographers get certified in scuba diving. Scuba gear lets people breathe underwater for around an hour at a time. Even with the gear, divers have to be careful about how deep they go. The pressure as they go deeper can be dangerous, and it can cause health problems if divers aren't careful. Experienced divers might be able to go down a few hundred feet, but that brings them just a fraction of the way down into the sunlight zone. To explore deeper, they need to use other methods.

When areas are too deep for people to safely explore, oceanographers use submersibles. A submersible is an underwater vehicle that's super strong to withstand the pressure of the ocean depths. But there isn't a person inside driving it. The submersible is connected to a larger boat or a lab on shore, and the driver uses a controller to move the submersible around. It's kind of like driving an underwater remote control car. Oceanographers can stay safe on the surface and look at video feeds to see what the submersible sees. Another way that oceanographers can explore deep waters is by using sonar, which is short for "sound navigation and ranging." From a boat on the surface, sonar sends sound waves into the ocean. The sound waves travel down, and when they bump into an object (like an animal), they bounce back up to the surface. Equipment on the ship lets the person reading it know how far away the object the sonar sensed is. This information can help with mapping the ocean and detecting things like shipwrecks hidden on the seafloor. Looking at the sea from outer space might sound absurd, but satellites are another important tool in ocean mapping. Using a satellite image gives scientists a very zoomed-out picture. It shows details you might not be able to see from up close. You can even see the Great Barrier Reef from the Moon!

WHAT'S IN THE WATER?

Ocean water isn't like the water in your bathtub or your sink, and it's very different from the water you'll find in ponds and lakes. All of that water is fresh water, but ocean water is salt water. And while a pond might be still and motionless on a calm day, the ocean never stops moving. That's because the ocean is controlled by tides, and the waves and currents in the water keep it constantly churning around.

SALTY SEAS

The salt in the water comes from the land. Rain and other natural elements erode the rock on the shore and along riverbanks. That means that the rain slowly breaks down the rocks, and the tiny bits mix into the water. The movement from the rivers into the ocean releases sodium chloride and dissolves it into the ocean. Sodium chloride is the chemical name for salt, just like the salt you would put on food.

BLUE LAGOONS

First things first, why are they blue? It's not actually the water that's blue. The ocean is blue because of sunlight. The sun beams down on the surface of the water in all different colors, but the water absorbs others (meaning you don't see them) and reflects some of the colors (meaning you do see them). The water absorbs colors like red, orange, and yellow from the sunlight, and it reflects blue back at you.

MOTION IN THE OCEAN

You might have heard the terms "high tide" and "low tide," and if you've ever been to the beach during them you can see (and smell) the difference. The tides are changes in sea level caused by gravitational forces from the Moon. At high tide, the water level at the beach is much higher, and you can see less of the sand. But at low tide a lot more of the sand is exposed and the water is much further out. At low tide, you can see things like tide pools in rocks, seashells on the beach, and clumps of seaweed left behind by the waves. Plus, low tide smells a lot worse.

There's nothing quite like the sound of waves crashing on a beach. But why are the waves in the ocean so much bigger than in other bodies of water? When energy passes through the water, it moves the water in a circular motion that creates a wave. The biggest form of energy that causes waves is wind. The wind blows against the surface of the water and creates friction. That means the wind and the water rub up against each other when they meet. That friction causes energy and creates waves. The movement of the ocean water is called a current. The water is constantly moving from one location to another because of tides and wind. Currents can bring warm water to cooler areas (or the other way around), and they can bring chemicals, things floating in the water, and boats and animals along with them as they move. The currents along the surface of the water are controlled by wind, and these surface currents are tracked using a system called gyres.

Deeper down in the ocean, currents are usually caused by different temperatures of water meeting. Remember, cold water sinks (see page 16), so when cold and warm water collide, the water shifts around. Currents can change when a natural disaster like an earthquake or volcano eruption shifts around the direction of the water. Some currents can move incredibly fast—these are called rip currents. Swimmers in the ocean need to be aware of rip currents. They can move at speeds of 8 feet (2.4 meters) per second. That's faster than an Olympic swimmer! Swimmers caught in rip currents can easily be pulled away from the shore or under the water. If you're ever caught in a rip current, the most dangerous thing to do is try to swim straight to shore in the opposite direction of the current. It's a lot stronger than you are, so you don't want to swim against it. Instead of fighting the current, you want to swim with it parallel to the shore and make your way back to land at an angle.

WEATHER AND WAVES

When the wind starts to rage, it can get treacherous on the water. Wind can turn into a storm, and when it starts blowing at more than 74 miles (120 kilometers) per hour it's called a hurricane. Hurricane winds can generate waves up to 60 feet (18.3 meters) high. Hurricanes create rough seas with intense winds and crashing waves. It's very dangerous to be out on the water, and hurricanes can easily hit and flood the coastline. Hurricanes aren't the only natural events that cause giant waves. Earthquakes and underwater volcanic eruptions can generate massive waves called tsunamis. Tsunamis are super-fast-moving waves; they can travel as fast as a jet plane. When tsunamis swell and crash, they can destroy marine habitats, flood the shore, and cause a lot of damage both in the water and on land.

TSUNAMI

The word *tsunami* means "harbor wave" in Japanese. And that's just what struck Japan on March 11, 2011. On that day, off the coast of Japan, a magnitude 9.1 earthquake—the fourth-strongest earthquake ever recorded—shook the ocean floor, more than 18 miles (29 kilometers) beneath the water's surface. That earthquake created a tsunami that moved at more than 400 miles (640 kilometers) per hour! Residents along the coast had just minutes of warning before the massive waves hit.

Have you ever seen a big wave that was moving fast, and ran away from it?

UNDERSEA GEOLOGY

Just like the land has mountains and valleys, the ocean has a very interesting landscape. The seafloor (or seabed) is at the very bottom of the ocean. In shallow areas, the seafloor is usually sandy and loose. As you get deeper, the seafloor gets thicker and more claylike. And in the deepest areas, the seafloor gets rocky with features like boulders. It makes sense when you think about it—boulders are a whole lot heavier than pebbles, which means they sink down and are much harder for waves and currents to move toward the shore.

One feature that marine geologists study are underwater mud volcanoes. On the ocean floor, mud volcanoes spew up gasses, minerals and, well, mud, from beneath the earth's crust. The volcanoes' contents mix with the seawater. Scientists don't know much about these geologic features, but they are fascinated by them. One reason why is that, somehow, microbial animals thrive in them! And if life can find a way in those conditions, scientists wonder if life can exist in similar conditions on other planets and moons, like Jupiter's moon, Europa.

TECTONIC PLATES

The outermost layer of Earth's crust is made up of tectonic plates—these plates are large pieces of rock that fit together like a giant puzzle, but the plates move slowly over time. And as the plates move, they can overlap or separate, causing things like earthquakes, mountains, and trenches. The slow movement of the tectonic plates changes the size and shape of the oceans and the continents around them.

THE CONTINENTAL SHELF

Extending out from the shore is a relatively shallow area. It gets a little bit deeper as you move further out, but the change in depth is gradual (it happens just a little bit at a time). Then, the ocean floor suddenly drops down into a much deeper area. The part of the seafloor before the drop is called the continental shelf. The drop is called the continental slope. The continental shelf gets its name because you'll find it around continents and islands. It's part of the sunlight zone, and it's usually filled with sea life. The continental slope is where you'll enter new depth zones (see pages 18-19).

The continental shelf is wider by some shorelines than others. For example, off the coast of Siberia, the continental shelf is very wide—more than 900 miles (1,450 kilometers) lie between the water's edge and the shelf break! In contrast, the continental shelf off the coast of northern California is just a few miles wide before the water gets very deep.

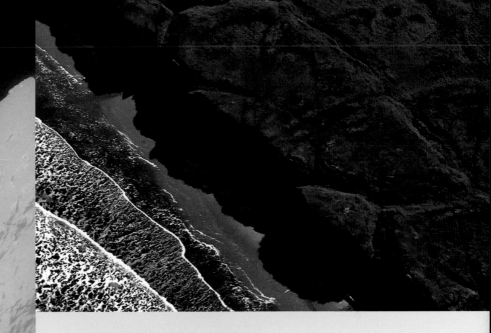

THE BERING LAND BRIDGE

The shelf to the east of Siberia was once above water. That's because, toward the end of the Ice Age, so much of the earth's water was frozen into glaciers that global sea levels were about 400 feet (121.9 meters) lower! To the east of the shelf, a wide, grassy "bridge" to a new continent appeared—the Bering Land Bridge. And scientists today believe that that's how the Americas—North America, Central America, and South America—came to be populated by humans. But it was a close call.

Based on new evidence, scientists now think that the Ice Age glaciers formed quickly, close to the end of the Ice Age. The Bering Land Bridge probably appeared about 37,500 years ago. That left about 27,000 years for primitive humans to find their way across the Bering Land Bridge, before it sank back underwater. And that's where it has been for the last 10,000 years!

What do you think convinced the early humans of Siberia to leave their homeland and travel eastward across the new land bridge?

THE ABYSSAL PLAINS

The abyssal plains are the largest area of the ocean, but they're not really plains like you would see on land. The abyssal plains aren't flat—they have valleys, hills, canyons, and seamounts breaking up the landscape. A seamount is what oceanographers call an underwater mountain. The abyssal plains can be anywhere from 10,000 to 20,000 feet (3,000 to 6,000 meters) below the surface, which means they're in both the midnight depth zone and the abyssal zone (see page 19). They're the largest habitat on the whole planet. In fact, the abyssal plains cover more than 50% of the Earth's surface.

The word "abyss" comes from the Ancient Greek word abyssos (ἄβυσσος), which means "bottomless" or "great depth."

Dirt, sand, and other sediments obey gravity and settle on abyssal plains, which is why they look like "plains." On average, the sediment collected on abyssal plains is a kilometer (0.6 miles) thick!

If you've ever waded through pond muck, how thick was that sediment? Now imagine it was over half a mile thick!

OCEAN TRENCHES

Trenches are long, narrow ditches. Ocean trenches are the deepest part of the ocean floor. These sharp drops break up the abyssal plains. The deepest known part of the ocean sits 36,201 feet (11,034 meters) below the surface in the Mariana Trench in the hadal zone (see page 19).

DEEPEST OF THE DEEP

In the southern end of the Mariana Trench is the Challenger Deep, the deepest known point on planet earth. In 2012, movie director James Cameron went by himself in the deep-submersible vehicle (DSV) Deepsea Challenger. His solo dive took him to 35,787 feet (10,908 meters—that's 6.77 miles, or 10.9 kilometers) deep! The movie he made over the course of that dive is called Deepsea Challenge. He was the third person to reach Challenger Deep (the first trip, in 1960, involved two people), and he inspired more explorers. Since 2019, one of the most impressive vehicles ever made, the DSV Limiting Factor, has gone to the Deep at least 19 times. The trip down takes four hours, most of it through pure darkness!

If you were offered a chance to go on the Limiting Factor, which has room for two people, would you take it?

SUBMARINE VOLCANOES

Water and lava might not sound like they go together, but underwater volcanoes, called submarine volcanoes, are pretty common. Some of the volcanoes are completely underwater. When fully submerged volcanoes erupt, it's not quite the dramatic explosion you would see from a volcano aboveground with lava shooting into the air. The volcano erupts into the water, which has a lot of pressure and keeps the lava from shooting up. Instead, the lava oozes out onto the seafloor. The lava hardens as it cools and sticks onto the volcano, making it a little bigger every time it erupts. The growth of the volcano, along with tectonic plate movement, can eventually bring the top of the volcano up above the surface of the water. These submarine volcanoes form islands, and you might recognize some of them. Hawaii, Indonesia, and Iceland are all examples of islands that were formed from submarine volcanoes. In fact, the tallest mountain on Earth is actually mostly underwater. Mauna Kea on the Big Island of Hawaii is a total of 33,500 feet (10,211 meters) tall, but 19,700 feet (6,000 meters) of its height is under the water. Mount Everest, in comparison, is 29,035 feet (8,850 meters) in total, but it reaches a much higher elevation (height above sea level) than Mauna Kea because its base is on land.

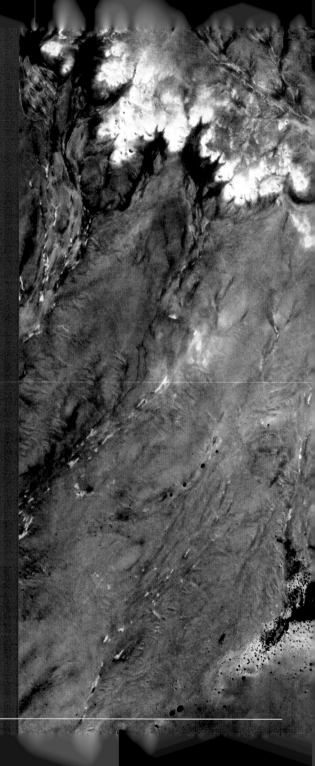

More than 80 percent of volcano eruptions happen underwater. So, how do scientists find them and track them? They use pictures taken by satellites in orbit, combined with computer programs that constantly analyze the pictures, to look for different colors in the water. They also measure how much sulfur dioxide is in clouds.

MID-OCEAN RIDGES

Mid-ocean ridges are underwater mountain ranges. Deep below the surface, you'll find the longest mountain range on Earth at over 40,000 miles (64,000 kilometers) long. This mid-ocean ridge is made up of volcanoes that run along the seafloor.

How does a mid-ocean ridge form? Basically, it's the exact opposite of how regular mountains form. Instead of two tectonic plates—sections of the earth's crust—smashing together and pushing each other up into a mountain range, seamounts in the mid-ocean ridge are created when tectonic plates pull apart. When the plates pull apart, magma spews up from the gap. The ocean cools down the magma and that's how the seamount is made! The slower the magma escapes, the steeper the seamount's slopes are.

HYDROTHERMAL VENTS

Hydrothermal vents are a unique part of the underwater landscape. They're kind of like underwater hot springs. You'll find hydrothermal vents at mid-ocean ridges with submarine volcanoes. The vents are breaks in the seafloor where cold water can travel through to the magma in a submarine volcano. The water heats up, then comes back up through the vent. Even though most of the water at these depths would be freezing cold, water coming up through hydrothermal vents can reach over 700 degrees Fahrenheit (370 degrees Celsius)— that's hot enough to melt solid metal! When the water and magma meet, it also makes chemical changes to the water that are unlike the conditions found in any other location in the ocean. The combination of the water chemistry and temperature makes hydrothermal vents a super-special environment with life-forms that couldn't exist anywhere else.

The discovery of hydrothermal vents in 1977 was a big deal. Before scientists finally saw these vents in action, off the coast of the Galapagos Islands, we were sure that all life depended on the availability of sunlight. But this discovery proved otherwise. Crabs, tubeworms, microbes—all kinds of animals find living by hydrothermal vents just as good as life in the sun!

ENVIRONMENTS AND ECOSYSTEMS

We've already talked about hydrothermal vents (see page 37), but there are lots of other unique environments and ecosystems in the ocean. Environments, or habitats, are surroundings where plants and animals live. The plants and animals in any environment interact with each other, and with the environment around them. These interactions in a particular habitat make up an ecosystem.

Here are some examples of ocean ecosystems and what lives in them:

The **intertidal zone**—mangrove swamps. While the tide brings ocean water ashore, it also pulls the water back out. The mangrove tree lives in this zone, using its fingerlike roots to grab hold of the sandy soil. Aquatic birds like pelicans and anhinga make nests in mangrove canopies, while crabs and reptiles live in the tangled roots below, and starfish and shellfish live in the shallow water.

The **benthic zone**—coral reefs. On the seafloor under shallow water, approximately one-quarter of all ocean species depend on coral reefs for food and shelter (see page 42).

The **pelagic zone**—open ocean. The water's temperature changes with wind patterns and currents, and seaweed and plankton grows here, absorbing sunlight near the surface. Whales and dolphins love the open ocean, as do many other large, migratory fish.

The **abyssal zone**—deep ocean. It's cold and dark here, and the weight of all the water above means that animals without bones—invertebrates—and microorganisms are mostly what you'll find. Where sunlight is scarce, these animals turn to another source of food—chemicals and minerals spewing from vents in the ocean floor—for survival.

TURTLE GRASS

Under the warm water up to 30 feet (9.1 meters) deep in the Gulf of Mexico, turtle grass forms gently waving grassy seabeds. Blades of turtle grass that separate flow into the abyssal plains, where they sink and become food for deep-sea animals. But sadly, farm chemicals flowing from the Mississippi River are causing the turtle grass plains to shrink!

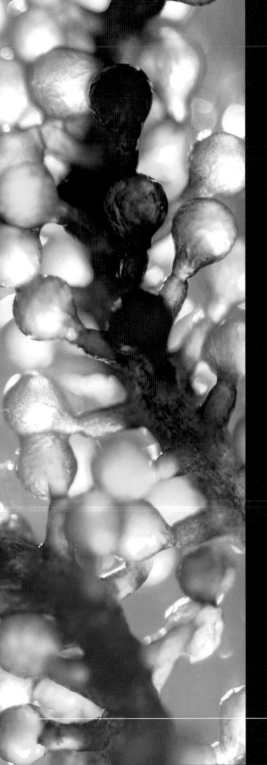

PLANTS AND PLANKTON

Some of the most important life-forms in the ocean are the smallest. There are lots of fish and large animals in the ocean, but they all need food to survive. On land, plenty of large animals are herbivores. That means they eat plants, and on land that can mean grass, leaves, flowers, or any other plants. The seafloor doesn't have grass, but there's still plenty of plants for herbivores to eat. There are countless species of plants growing in the water, and they're most often called seaweed. Seaweed can be small, like tiny algae, or huge, like giant kelp. Seaweed is an important source of food for lots of different animals.

On land there are many animals that eat insects (insectivores), other small animals (carnivores), or both plants and animals (omnivores). You won't find flying insects under the water, but there are plenty of small organisms like crustaceans and plankton that act as the "bugs" of the ocean. Plankton are drifting organisms in the ocean that float along with the current. There are two different types of plankton: phytoplankton and zooplankton. Phytoplankton are plants, like algae, and zooplankton are animals, like krill. The group "plankton" fits together because these organisms are all drifters. That means they can't really swim; they just rely on the current to move them. That makes them a perfect source of food for fish, whales, and other marine animals. Most plankton can't swim for their entire lives. But some species just drift when they're young, and eventually learn how to swim when they get older. Usually plankton are less than an inch in size, but some crustaceans and jellyfish are actually considered plankton.

REEFS

Coral reefs are one of the biggest habitats in the ocean, and they have some of the most interesting wildlife you'll see. About 25% of all ocean species live in the warm, shallow water around coral reefs. It's easy to mistake coral for a rock, but it's an animal species. One big piece of coral is actually made up of tiny, individual coral bits called polyps. All of the polyps put together are what you see when you look at a piece of coral. Oceanographers call this type of animal behavior a colonial organism, because the polyp colony is what makes up the coral.

Coral reefs are made up of thousands of pieces of coral, and the coral get its food from algae that grows on it. The algae needs the coral, too. Without it, the algae wouldn't have a home. The coral and the algae both rely on each other to stay alive—this kind of relationship is called mutualism. The algae is what gives the coral reef its color. Coral can look blue, green, pink, or red, depending on the algae that lives on it. If the water around coral gets too warm or too polluted, the coral turns white. The algae that lives on the coral (and gives it color) can't survive, and when it dies the color on the coral goes away. But that means that the coral is missing its main food source, which can kill the coral. Coral turning white is called coral bleaching. It puts the whole reef at risk. If the coral can't survive, then neither can the plants and animals that live around it.

The largest coral reef in the world is called the Great Barrier Reef. This reef sits on the seafloor off the coast of Australia, where thousands of reefs are connected in a chain over 1,400 miles (2,250 kilometers) long. This reef has been there for thousands of years, but climate change and pollution have killed about half of the coral in the reef since 2016.

All corals are sessile, which means they are permanently attached to the ocean floor or other corals.

There are three types of reefs: barrier, atoll, and fringing. Fringing reefs, the most common, grow right along the land. Barrier reefs are separated from land by deep lagoons. Atoll reefs are formed when a fringing reef growing around an island or volcano top keeps growing after the island sinks.

SEA FAN CORAL

DAISY CORAL

BRAIN CORAL

STAGHORN CORAL

GOLF BALL CORAL

ORGAN PIPE CORAL

KELP FORESTS

Kelp is a type of seaweed that can grow super fast. Sometimes it can grow over 1 foot (0.3 meters) in a day! Tall kelp can grow together to form kelp forests. You'll usually find kelp forests in cold, shallow water. Many species make their home in kelp forests. The kelp is a great source of food, and it also makes for a much safer home than the open water. The kelp can work as camouflage, and smaller animals use it to hide from large predators. Some species, like sea otters, will even use the kelp as an anchor. They can hang onto the kelp or wrap it around young otters to make sure that nobody drifts away while they're resting.

URCHINS

Spiky creatures called purple sea urchins love to eat kelp.

BULL KELP

This kind of kelp looks like a bull whip, with a long, leafless stalk ending in a floating bulb, from which a bunch of long, wavy leaves grows. The stalk, known as the stipe, can grow up to about 60 feet (18.3 meters) long. The bulb, called a pneumatocyst because it's an air-filled sac that serves as a floatation device, can be almost 5 inches (12.7 centimeters) across.

Bull kelp forests grow off the Pacific coast of North America, where they have a symbiotic relationship with sea otters. Sea otters use the forests as protection and cover, and in return, they eat up the urchins that would devour the forest if there were too many of them.

PINK CONCH

KEYHOLE LIMPET

RAZOR CLAM

HORSE CONCH

SAND DOLLAR

SCALLOP

COCKLE

COWRY

BEACHES AND SHALLOWS

Not all ocean animals spend their time underwater. There are plenty of species that spend some time on land, which makes beaches and shallow water areas an important part of their environment. Some beaches are made up of rocks, shells, or tiny bits of minerals. Others are made up of sand. Sand is a super-important part of the environment. Some species, like mussels and clams, burrow down under the sand. And some animals, like turtles, lay their eggs in the sand. Other beaches have dunes and beach grass, which are helpful for food and shelter.

Beaches and shallows are constantly changing because of the tides. The shoreline will look very different between high and low tides. When the tide goes out, it sometimes reveals tide pools. Tide pools are small collections of water that you would find in places like rock crevices. When the tide is high, it completely covers the tide pool with water. But when the tide is low, the area around the tide pool is exposed. There are some organisms, like barnacles, that spend their entire life in tide pools. But there are also some that come and go with the changing tides. During low tide, tide pools become self-contained ecosystems. The only food available is what is already in the tide pool, and they're exposed to much more sun and wind than they would be at high tide. Animals that can only travel in the water will be stuck in the tide pool until high tide, when the water level gets high enough for them to leave.

OCEAN CLIMATES

Just like on land, the climate of the ocean changes depending on where you are on the globe. In places that are near the equator and warm year-round, the water is also usually warm. These are called tropical oceans. In areas around the North and South Poles, where it's usually cold or snowy, the water is also cold and is often frozen. These are called polar oceans. The types of plants and animals you'll find in tropical oceans and polar oceans are very different. That's because plants and animals will adapt to live in a certain climate to help them stay warm or cool. And what helps them in one climate doesn't always help them in another, making it difficult for them to survive anywhere but home.

There are some animals that travel long distances from their home. They'll pass through different areas and climates as they move. These long travels are called migrations. Animals migrate for a lot of different reasons. Sometimes, it's to find food, and other times it's to breed in a certain location. Humpback whales are one example—they migrate from colder climates to warmer climates to give birth to their young. Sea turtles will migrate in search of their favorite food: jellyfish. Some animals will follow the same migration path every time they travel. Migrations can take animals across thousands of miles of ocean.

Oceans do an amazing job at absorbing heat. What that means, unfortunately, is that oceans are warming much faster than land from the effects of climate change. Over the last 120 years, the average temperature near the ocean's surface has gone up by 1.5 degrees Fahrenheit (0.8 degrees Celsius), and most of that increase has happened in just the last three decades! What does that mean for sea animals? They're moving! Most of the world's ocean life is migrating to new areas for food and breeding due to climate change.

THE AQUATIC FOOD CHAIN

Oceanographers know that hundreds of thousands of different species live in the ocean, and there are probably a lot more than they've seen. Scientists think that 90% of ocean species haven't been classified yet, so the real number of species that live in the ocean is unknown. With so many animals living together, a food chain forms. Food chains are ways for scientists to understand how species in the same habitat rely on one another. The lowest level of the food chain is a food source for the level above it, and so on. When multiple food chains overlap in the same environment, it's called a food web. Let's take a look at five levels of ocean food chains.

PRIMARY PRODUCERS

These organisms create their own food using a process called photosynthesis. Photosynthesis uses energy from the sun to make food to keep the organism alive. Some examples of primary producers in the ocean are seaweed and phytoplankton.

PRIMARY CONSUMERS

The next step in the food chain is primary consumers, and they eat primary producers. Some examples of primary consumers in the ocean are zooplankton, crustaceans, and mollusks.

SECONDARY CONSUMERS

The secondary consumers eat the primary consumers, and some examples in the ocean are fish and crabs. But even some larger creatures can be secondary consumers. Whales that eat krill (a type of zooplankton) are also secondary consumers.

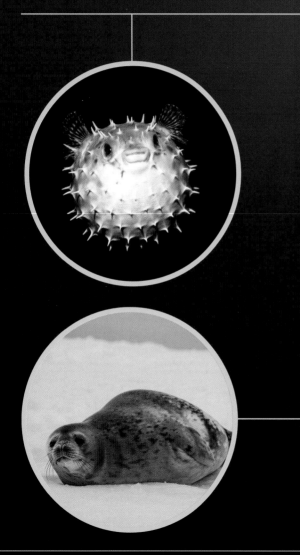

TERTIARY CONSUMERS

Tertiary consumers are predators; they hunt and eat smaller animals. Ocean tertiary consumers include seals, octopuses, and bigger fishes (like tuna).

APEX PREDATORS

The apex means the top, and apex predators are at the top of the food chain. That means that they will hunt and eat anything below them on the food chain. Sharks and orcas are two ocean apex predators.

CIRCLE OF LIFE

The food chain might look like a straight line, but in reality it's more of a circle. Apex predators are at the top when they're alive, but when they die, they become a food source for organisms much lower on the food chain, like bacteria and scavengers. A scavenger is an animal that eats meat, but doesn't hunt for live animals. Instead, it looks for animals that are already dead. That way it gets food without a fight.

INVERTEBRATES

Invertebrates are a group of animals that don't have a spine. This group includes animals like snails, crustaceans, and mollusks. Marine invertebrates have been around for millions of years—they're some of the oldest animals on Earth. Let's look at a few groups of marine invertebrates that are key to ocean ecosystems.

ANEMONE

Bright colors and waving tentacles make anemones look like underwater flowers. But these plants have protection. Anemone tentacles can sting, which lets them paralyze prey. Anemones grow slowly and can live for 80 years.

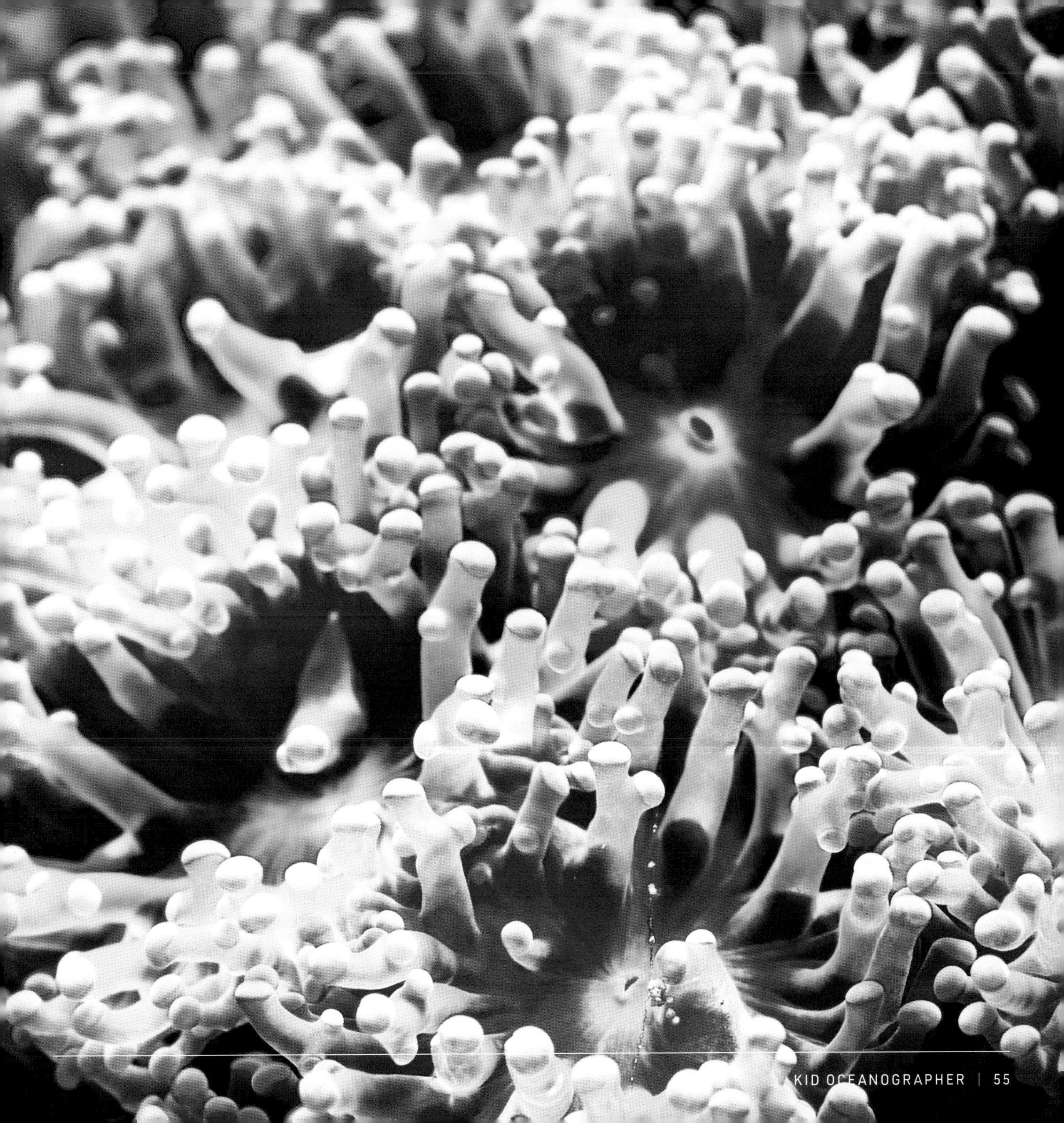

BARNACLE

They may not look like it, but barnacles are actually animals. They're crustaceans that stick onto surfaces like rocks, the bottoms of boats, or even the sides of whales. They stick to one spot for their entire life, and they eat by shooting appendages (growths that are like little arms or fingers) through an opening at the top of their shells.

You would think that barnacles have a lot in common with snails, but other than their shells, they don't. If you were to peek inside a barnacle's shell, you would see a crablike animal!

Have you ever tried to peel a barnacle off a surface before? It's not easy! That's because they stick to surfaces—whale and manatee bodies, dock posts, boat hulls—by secreting a natural glue substance that has an adhesive strength of 22 to 60 pounds per square inch (10 to 27 kilograms per 25 square mm).

CLAM

Clams are experts at digging holes in the sand. You'll find clams on beaches buried under the sand in holes as deep as 4 feet (1.2 meters). Clams make these sand burrows to hide from beach predators like birds.

Giant clams (genus *Tridacna*) grow to about 4 feet (1.2 meters) in length and over 400 pounds (180 kilograms). When they are very young, they find a comfy spot on a reef to attach themselves to, and there they stay, living as long as 100 years!

One reason they grow so big and live so long is because they have a symbiotic relationship—a relationship where both species benefit each other—with algae. The algae takes shelter in the giant clam's shell, and the clam can use the algae's waste products as food. Giant clams even open their shells during the day so their algae can absorb sunlight!

CRAB

Crustaceans are a group of animals with hard outer shells called exoskeletons. They're a bit like the "bugs" of the ocean. Crabs are a type of crustacean that you'll see a lot on beaches. They have wide bodies, two front pincer claws, and eight additional legs for walking across the sand. They usually walk sideways, because it's faster for them than moving forward. Hermit crabs are one species of crab that doesn't have its own hard exoskeleton—instead, they slide their bodies into old snail shells.

HORSESHOE CRAB

Horseshoe crabs aren't actually crabs at all! They're more closely related to arachnids, like spiders. What's amazing about them is that they've been on Earth for about 450 million years.

JAPANESE SPIDER CRAB

The Japanese Spider Crab is much bigger than most crabs. Some measure around 15 feet (4.6 meters) from claw to claw!

DECORATOR CRAB

Decorator Crabs camouflage themselves by sticking small objects like seaweed or rocks to their shells. Their shells are covered with bristles that work a lot like Velcro!

CUTTLEFISH

Compared to squids and octopuses, cuttlefish have larger, wider bodies and shorter legs. Cuttlefish are slow swimmers, but they're incredibly good at changing color. They're sometimes called the "chameleons of the sea." They can change color in just 1 second. The color change can be used to communicate with other cuttlefish, or it can be camouflage to hide from predators.

JELLYFISH

Jellyfish don't have jelly in their bodies, but they do have a lot of water. In fact, jellyfish are 95% water, and they don't have a brain, heart, or blood. Many jellyfish have stinging tentacles, like the lion's mane jellyfish and the Portuguese man o' war.

BIOLUMINESCENCE

Some jellyfish, like the beautiful crystal jelly, can glow in the dark. The incredible ability for some animals (like fireflies!) to make their own light is called bioluminescence. Bioluminescence comes from a chemical reaction in certain animals that lets off energy in the form of light.

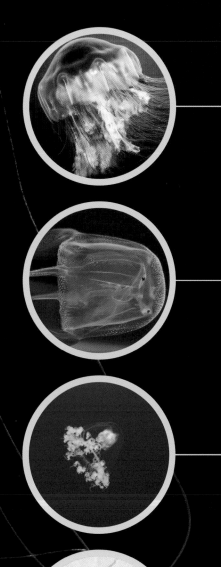

LION'S MANE

The lion's mane is the biggest known species of jellyfish. Its tentacles can grow up to 100 feet (30.5 meters) long!

BOX

Box jellyfish are one of the deadliest animals in the entire ocean. They have very powerful stingers on their tentacles. They're also some of the only jellyfish with the ability to swim; they can control both their direction and speed. And not only that—they can see, too!

TURRITOPSIS DOHRNII

The Turritopsis dohrnii is a tiny and especially fascinating kind of jellyfish. When it's injured, it goes back into an earlier stage of its development—in a way, it gets younger! This amazing ability has led some scientists to nickname it "the immortal jellyfish."

PORTUGUESE MAN O' WAR

The Portuguese man o' war looks like a jellyfish, but technically, it isn't one—in fact, it's not even one animal! Each man o' war is a collection of individual tiny creatures called a *superorganism*.

KRILL

Krill are one of the most important animals in the ocean ecosystem. They're a type of zooplankton, and they're the main source of food for animals like whales, fish, and penguins. Krill are a type of small crustacean that can be found all over the world. They travel in swarms and can live for ten years.

LOBSTER

Another crustacean, lobsters have long bodies with a hard shell. Over time, the lobster sheds its shell and grows a new one. This helps keep the shell hard, and they'll do it several times in their lives. They have fan-shaped tails that help them swim and powerful claws that are good for crushing prey.

NAUTILUS

Species of nautilus have existed on Earth for 500 million years. The nautilus has a spiral shell on its back that's filled with gas. The nautilus moves like a submarine. The gas helps it to lift up or sink down in the water.

OCTOPUS

The octopus has suckers on the bottom of each of its eight arms that it can use to grip onto things. Octopuses don't have any bones, and they can fold their bodies to fit in super-small spaces. Plus, they're incredibly smart—some can open latches or navigate mazes. Their bendy bodies and big brains make them escape artists. They also have a great defense system. When they're threatened, they can change color or shoot ink, and they're even venomous. An octopus will only mate once in its life. When a female lays eggs, she stays and guards them for months. The mother dies soon after the eggs hatch.

OYSTER

An oyster's hard shell serves as protection for the squishy body inside. That protection is important, because oysters stay in one place for their entire lives. Oysters have the special ability to produce pearls.

SCALLOP

Scallops use their fan-shaped shells to swim. They open and close the shell to move through the water. Scallops don't have a brain, but they do have eyes along the edge of their shell , which help them sense predators.

SPANISH DANCER

ANNA'S SEA SLUG

VERICOSE SEA SLUG

SEA SLUG

There are some sea slugs that resemble their land-based relatives. But one group of sea slugs is a lot more colorful than land slugs. This slug is called the nudibranch (see examples to the left here), and its color serves as a warning to predators—this slug is poisonous!

SEA SNAIL

Just like snails on land, sea snails have coiled shells. They're part of a group called mollusks, which also includes animals like mussels, oysters, and scallops. Mollusks have hard outer shells covering soft, blobby bodies.

SEA SPONGE

Sea sponges are a lot like the ones you use to clean your dishes. There are thousands of sea sponge species, and they've been around for millions of year. Sea sponges don't have stomachs, brains, or hearts. Instead, they eat using a method called filtering. They have tiny, hairlike structures in their bodies that trap food and filter out bacteria and seawater.

BARREL SPONGE

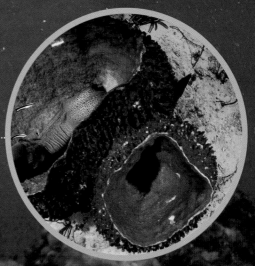

AZURE VASE SPONGE

SEA STAR

You'll sometimes hear sea stars be called "starfish," but they aren't really a fish at all. Sea stars are part of a group of animals called echinoderms. Sea stars can have anywhere from 5 to 40 arms. The arms have tiny feet on the bottom that allow the sea stars to walk, and each arm has an eye at the end. If one of the arms is injured, the sea star can grow it back.

SHRIMP

Shrimp have ten legs, and they mostly travel by swimming. Shrimp have long antennae coming out of their heads. Their eyes are attached to their head with stalks, and they have very good eyesight. Shrimp can be small, but there are also some species that grow to be a foot long. One kind of shrimp, the mantis shrimp, is a predator that uses its claws like a spear to catch small fish.

MANTIS SHRIMP

SQUID

Squids look a little bit like octopuses.
They have legs that come straight out of
their bodies. But squids have much more
slender bodies than octopuses. Squids
are super speedy, and when they travel,
they move in groups called schools.

URCHIN

The ball-shaped urchin is covered in sharp spines. The spines are a form of protection that helps keep the urchins safe from predators. Urchins can be all kinds of bright colors, like purple or red. One type of urchin, the sand dollar, is often found washed up on beaches.

PURPLE URCHIN

RED URCHIN

FIRE URCHIN

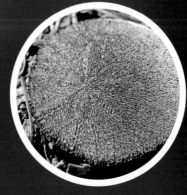

SAND DOLLAR

FISH

Small or large, camouflaged or colored, fish can come in just about every shape, size, and color. Unlike invertebrates, fish are vertebrate animals, which means they have a spine. Fish live in the water and breathe through gills. They don't have fingers or toes, but they do have fins to help them swim. They usually have scales and lay eggs, and most fish are cold-blooded. That means that they rely on the environment around them to keep them warm or cool them down.

Fish first evolved about 530 million years ago, in the early Cambrian period—that's 300 million years before the dinosaurs appeared! Fish have been around for a long, long time, so of course they have evolved in many different ways. In fact, of all the different kinds of vertebrates—animals with backbones—half are fish!

Even today, scientists are still discovering new fish. In 2023, off the coast of Costa Rica, they found a new kind of fish: a lavender-colored, eel-like one about 6 inches (15.2 centimeters) long, living near a hydrothermal vent a mile deep. They called it *Pyrolycus jaco*, after the Costa Rican city of Jacó. It's a new species of eelpout, which is a family of slimy, pouty-looking fish!

Let's take a look at some of the fish you might see swimming through the sea.

ANGELFISH

An angelfish has a very recognizable body shape. It's incredibly flat, and it has long, pointed fins on the top and bottom of its body. Angelfish can come in all sizes and colors. Many types of angelfish even have stripes or spots on their bodies. One species, the queen angelfish, is common in reefs. It has a bright blue-and-yellow body, and it eats sea sponges.

There are angelfishes that live in freshwater (not salty) environments, and there are many more angelfishes that live in marine (saltwater) environments. The freshwater kinds live in slow-moving sections of rivers in South America.

BALLOONFISH

You might have heard this fish be called a pufferfish or a porcupine fish. It has spines all over its body that are normally flat. When it's scared or threatened, the balloonfish puffs up its body. The body looks up to three times bigger, and the spines stick out all around it, making the balloonfish look a whole lot larger and more intimidating. But if a predator still decides to come closer, many species of balloonfish have a backup attack—their spines are venomous.

Have you noticed that balloonfish have big eyes? That's because they are nocturnal! During the day, they hide out in reef caves. At night, they come out to look for food, like unsuspecting hermit crabs.

BARRACUDA

Barracudas are hunters, and they prefer to go out hunting alone. These large fish have slender bodies and can swim very quickly. They also have a mouth full of sharp, pointed teeth to easily catch their prey.

The great barracuda (*Sphyraena barracuda*) can grow up to more than 5 feet (1.5 meters) long and swim up to 36 miles (58 kilometers) per hour—that's a fast-moving predator!

BUTTERFLY FISH

Butterfly fish look a little bit like a small angelfish. These tropical fish are usually only a few inches long, and they have thin, flat bodies that are perfect for weaving through coral. They're usually brightly colored, and they have markings on their bodies that look like what you might see on the wings of a butterfly.

When a coral reef is home to a thriving population of butterflyfishes, that means the reef is healthy and in good shape. While not all butterflyfishes live in coral reefs, most do. In fact, some butterflyfishes can only eat coral—they're called "obligate corallivores"!

CLOWNFISH

Clownfish are some of the most recognizable fish in the ocean. They usually have an orange body with large white stripes. Sometimes clownfish are called anemonefish because they like to live in areas with a lot of anemones (see page 54). The relationship between clownfish and anemones is called mutualism, because both species benefit from it. They both protect the other from predators and help to feed one another.

The clownfish's bright colors attract would-be predators to the anemones, and the anemones grab and eat these fish. The clownfish eats the leftovers, and its feces gives the anemones additional nutrients. But somehow, no one really knows how clownfishes aren't also killed by anemones' poisons!

COD

These greenish-or reddish-brown fish have rounded fins on the top and bottom of their body. Cod are predators that eat other fish and eels. The two most common types of cod are Atlantic cod and Pacific cod. Both are found in the northern parts of the ocean in cool, deep water.

There used to be more Atlantic cod swimming off the coast of New England and eastern Canada—a lot more. In the last 170 years, their numbers have decreased by over 90 percent! What do you think caused this population decline?

EEL

You might think eels look like snakes, with their long, winding bodies, but if you look closely, you'll see that eels have small fins. Moray eels look especially snakelike, with a mouth full of sharp, pointed teeth. Moray eels are very high up on the ocean food chain. They eat fish, crab, and octopuses, and there aren't many predators that are willing to hunt down a moray eel.

Eels come in a huge variety of shapes and sizes. The one-jawed eel is tiny—just 2 inches (5 centimeters) long—while the giant moray eel, the longest of all eels, grows up to 13 feet (4 meters) long. But the moray is skinny; the eels you have to watch out for are the conger eels, which can grow to weigh over 200 pounds (90 kilograms). They lurk in sunken shipwrecks and coastal waters, and have been known to take a bite out of unsuspecting divers! Generally, however, eels are perfectly kind creatures.

FLOUNDER

This flatfish spends a lot of its time lying on the ocean floor. It has a sand-colored body that helps it to blend in. Instead of having one eye on each side of its head, flounders have both eyes on the same side of their body. This allows them to lay totally flat on the seafloor for the ultimate camouflage.

Flounders have special cells called chromatophores that help them camouflage themselves. These cells can help the flounder's skin become brighter or darker, depending on where the flounder wants to hide.

GOBY

The goby likes to eat seaweed that grows on coral, but there are a lot of predators in reefs, and gobies are tiny fish. To stay safe, many gobies burrow into the sand or mud, and some will share their burrows with other animals.

In North America, the round goby (*Neogobius melanostomus*) is an unwelcome guest, arriving from Europe in the ballast water—water stored in ships, hulls to keep them balanced—of cargo ships. But that's just one species of goby out of more than 2,000!

GROUPER

The large-mouthed grouper looks like it's always frowning. These predators are large, but they're not as fast as some other fish species. They are good at sensing prey, so they bring a buddy when they hunt. Groupers and moray eels will hunt together. The grouper will hunt out prey in rocky areas and alert the eel to where they found it. Then the eel can wriggle into the rock and chase out the prey. Both the grouper and the eel get a meal out of the deal.

Yellowmouth groupers (*Mycteroperca interstitialis*) have an usual characteristic—they are protogynous hermaphrodites. They all begin their lives as females. But then, the ones who live to be more than 5 years old change into males!

LIONFISH

The orange-and-white lionfish has fan-shaped fins that give it the look of a lion's mane. Its bright colors are a warning to predators. The lionfish has large, venomous spines running down its back. These spines are super effective, and humans who are stung by lionfish spines can get very sick.

While they are beautiful for us to look at, lionfishes are pretty scary to about 50 other kinds of fish living in coral reef environments. They swim slowly but use their wavy, lion mane–like fins to corner their prey.

MANDARINFISH

The brightly colored mandarinfish is usually found in warm waters in the Pacific Ocean. It has a bold blue body with neon green and orange markings. These small fish usually stay near the ocean floor to feed, and they tend to be found hunting around reefs for small crustaceans and invertebrates.

Not only are mandarinfishes toxic, they're stinky! They have cells in their skin that secrete a mucus coating to protect it, and other cells that make this mucus coating toxic. This coating is said to smell really bad.

MARLIN

The spear-snouted marlin has long been a fisherman's foe. The Atlantic blue marlin can reach sizes of 16 feet (4.9 meters) long and 1,800 pounds (816.5 kilograms), making this huge fish a beast for fisherman to catch. In fact, a marlin was a main character battling a fishermen in Ernest Hemingway's *The Old Man and the Sea*.

Blue marlins are world travelers, always heading for warmer waters. One individual marlin was tagged—scientists put a small tracking device on it—off the Atlantic coast of America, then turned up later in the Indian Ocean!

RAY

Sea rays are a type of fish called cartilaginous fish, which means that their skeleton is cartilage (a tough type of tissue) instead of bones. Rays have wide, flat bodies with long, pointed tails. They swim using the fins at the sides of their bodies, and those fins are connected directly to their heads. The stingray is a type of ray that has a venomous stinger in its tail, kind of like the stinger of a bee. It uses the stinger for defense—the stinger breaks off after the stingray uses it so that it can swim away. Another type of ray, the manta ray, is known for its massive size. Manta rays can grow to be 20 feet (6.1 meters) long.

GIANT MANTA RAY

BLUE-SPOTTED RIBBONTAIL RAY

PARROTFISH

Parrotfish are herbivores that play an interesting role in coral reef ecosystems. They eat algae that grows inside the coral, but to get to it they have to crunch through the coral using their parrotlike beak. The sounds of parrotfish eating coral are so loud you can hear it if you're under the water. Parrotfish break down a lot of the coral, but they send the bits of coral back into the ecosystem by pooping it out. Those bits actually make up white sand! Some species, like the rainbow parrotfish, have brilliant colors.

There are some kinds of parrotfish that make see-through sleeping bags for themselves. They secrete a mucus-y substance that they use to keep small bugs away while they sleep!

SEA DRAGON

Sea dragons live around Australia, but it's tough to see them out in the wild. They have excellent camouflage. Flaps of skin coming off their bodies look like leaves, which can help them to blend into their surroundings. The flaps move around in the water like floating seaweed, disguising the sea dragon.

SEAHORSE

The head and neck of a seahorse look like those of horses you might see on land, but a seahorse is indeed a type of fish. It uses its long snout to suck up food. Seahorses swim upright, and sometimes they'll use their long, curling tails as an anchor. The tail is prehensile, which means it can grasp onto things. Seahorses have some of the most interesting ways of giving birth of any animal. For most species, it's the female that gets pregnant and lays eggs to hatch. But male seahorses are the ones to get pregnant. Male seahorses have a special pouch on their bodies where females deposit eggs. Then the male carries the eggs around in the pouch until they hatch, and tiny little seahorses come out of the pouch.

PYGMY SEAHORSE

THORNY SEAHORSE

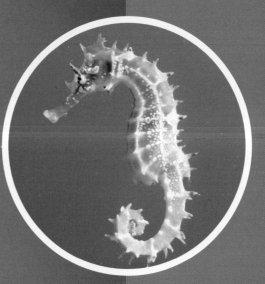

SHARK

Like rays, sharks are part of the group called cartilaginous fish. Many sharks are the apex predators of their ecosystem, and it's easy to see why. Sharks have a mouth full of teeth, and they're replaceable. That means that when the teeth fall out, the shark grows more. Some sharks, like the megamouth shark, are filter feeders. They suck enormous amounts of seawater into their mouths and filter out the food. But many other species of sharks are predators, and they're some of the most feared creatures in the ocean. The great white shark, tiger shark, and bull shark are truly terrifying creatures. They'll eat just about any smaller animal they encounter, and all three have been known to attack humans. Sharks have been around for about 400 million years, and today there are hundreds of different species. There are some small species that are only a few feet (and even a few inches!) long, and there are others, like the whale shark, that can grow to be 40 feet (12.2 meters) long.

TIGER SAND SHARK

GREENLAND SHARK

LEOPARD SHARK

GREAT WHITE SHARK

SHORT-FIN SHARK

WHALE SHARK

HAMMERHEAD SHARK

SURGEONFISH

Surgeonfish like to swim together in groups called schools. That means that all of the fish in the group swim together in the same direction. The school of fish is very coordinated, and it helps to protect individuals from predators. Surgeonfish like to eat seaweed and algae, and they have sharp spines on their tails. One of the most recognizable surgeonfish is the blue tang. It has a bright blue body with black markings and a yellow tail.

SWORDFISH

The swordfish is a predator with a built-in weapon. Its long, pointed snout can be used like a sword, slashing at prey to injure it or slow it down. The swordfish also has a streamlined body so that it can swim faster. Instead of scales, it has smooth skin.

TUNA

The tuna is a warm-water fish that's one of the fastest around. The yellowfin tuna can reach speeds over 45 miles (72.4 kilometers) per hour! Tunas are one of the only types of fish that can keep their bodies warmer than the water around them.

REPTILES AND BIRDS

Not every ocean animal spends its entire life in the water. Animals that spend part of their time on the shore are just as important to ocean ecosystems. Reptiles are closely related to fish—they are vertebrate animals (they have a spine), they have scaly skin, and they're usually cold-blooded. But reptiles breathe air, unlike fish, and they spend a lot of time on land. Birds are another key player in ocean life. They live on the beach, fly over the sea, and often eat fish and other ocean animals to stay alive.

There are more than 10,000 different species of reptiles. Remarkably resilient animals, reptiles have made it through not just one mass extinction event but three! The first was the Permian-Triassic event 250 million years ago, which killed off 90 percent of the earth's species. Reptiles also survived the most recent one, the Cretaceous-Paleogene event, which famously ended the age of the dinosaurs. So, as you might expect, the reptiles that survived to today can do amazing things. For instance, sea turtles can dive to about 900 feet (274.3 meters) deep before they need to come back up for air. That's like diving to the bottom of the deep end of the pool...times 75!

Here are some of the reptiles and birds that help out ocean ecosystems.

CROCODILE

The saltwater crocodile is a massive reptile you'll find in swampy coastal areas of India, Southeast Asia, and Australia. This crocodile prefers to live in mangroves, swamps, or river deltas. These areas have what's called brackish water—this kind of water has more salt than fresh water, but less salt than seawater, and it's common in locations where fresh water and ocean water meet (like where a river meets the ocean). These apex predators eat fish and crustaceans, along with birds, mammals, and other reptiles.

Saltwater crocodiles not only survived the last mass extinction event (the one that killed the dinosaurs 66 million years ago), they took the crown as earth's largest reptile. The biggest one ever recorded was Lolong, a deadly, man-eating croc who lived in the Phillipines and grew to over 20 feet (6.1 meters) long!

MARINE IGUANA

You'll only find marine iguanas on the Galápagos Islands, where this reptile lives on the shore and basks in the sun on rocks. The marine iguana is able to dive into the water to hunt for food, and most of its diet is algae.

When Charles Darwin took his famous voyage to the Galapagos Islands in the 1840s, there was one animal that he really didn't have many nice things to say about. When describing the marine iguanas he saw, he wrote that they were "hideous looking" and "disgusting, clumsy lizards." What do you think about their appearance?

SEA TURTLE

Sea turtles look a little bit different than turtles you would see on land. Instead of clawed feet, sea turtles have flippers, which help them to swim. Sea turtles lay their eggs buried in sand holes on beaches, and they can lay up to 100 eggs at a time. Some sea turtles will migrate (see page 48) incredibly long distances across the ocean to lay their eggs or hunt for food. Sea turtles don't have teeth, but they do have very powerful jaws.

When sea turtles migrate—and they are some of the most migratory animals on earth—they can swim about 20 miles (32 kilometers) per day! How far do you think you could swim in a day?

ALBATROSS

The albatross has the biggest wingspan of any bird at 11 feet (3.4 meters) across. And this bird needs those super-sized wings to stay in the air. The albatross flies out over the ocean, and sometimes when it travels it needs to fly for days, or even weeks, at a time.

The oldest known wild bird in history is a Laysan albatross (*Phoebastria immutabilis*) named Wisdom. She hatched in 1951! Scientists estimate that she has flown over 3 million miles (almost 5 million kilometers) in her lifetime.

AUK

Auks have unique wings that give them the ability to "fly" underwater. They're incredible divers and fast swimmers. They can dive over 300 feet (90 meters) deep, and they can swim fast enough to easily catch fish.

Auks, including puffins (see page 113, are pelagic birds, which means they spend most of their time out over the open ocean. That sounds tiring, but they are perfectly content resting on waves!

BLUE-FOOTED BOOBY

These birds live on rocky coasts in tropical areas of the Pacific Ocean. They get their name from their bright blue feet. This fish-eating bird dives under the water and can swim after its prey. It often starts the dive from very high up in the air, dramatically swooping down to the water.

To find mates, male blue-footed boobys have to show off their totipalmate—meaning that all four toes are connected by webbing—feet, and to show off their feet, they dance! The most popular males are the ones with the bluest feet.

HERON

Herons are most common in marshy areas or along the coast. They're recognizable by their long necks and long, skinny legs. They can't swim, so instead they stand in shallow water and stay completely still. They wait for prey like fish to swim by, then snatch it out of the water using their spear-like bill.

Herons have nesting areas that they use generation after generation, called "heronries," where it's possible to spot dozens of nests high up in the trees. Herons make some strange noises, including a prehistoric-sounding squawk. What do you think it sounds like at a heronry?

PELICAN

The big pouch on a pelican's throat works like a built-in net. They have long beaks with a pouch of skin on their throat. They use their bills and pouches to skim along the surface of the water and scoop up fish.

Brown pelicans, common on American coasts, catch food in a unique way. They fly up to 100 feet (30.5 meters) over the ocean and, using their fantastic vision, spot a fish in the water below. Then, tucking their wings back, they dive-bomb the fish. The force of impact often stuns the fish, making it easy to scoop it up!

PENGUIN

Penguins are a lot better at being in the water than in the air. Unlike other birds, penguins can't fly. Instead of wings, they have flippers. They're amazing divers, and they can swim so well it looks like they're flying under the water. Most penguins live in polar locations, so they have a thick coat of feathers and a layer of fat to keep them warm in the frigid waters. Penguins eat krill, fish, and squid, and they can spend weeks at sea when they're hunting for food. But when it's time to mate and lay eggs, penguins make their way back to land. Once they make it to shore, they live with other penguins in huge colonies.

PLOVER

You can find plovers all over the world, and they're a type of bird called wading birds. These are birds that you'll find along the shore. They wade into the water, usually to hunt for food. Some species of plovers burrow down into the sand.

Piping plovers, common along the Atlantic coast of North America, have a funny behavioral tic. If a human beachgoer ventures into the plover's territory, the plover will chaperone the human. It will keep an eye on the human and walk along with them until the beachgoer leaves its territory. Have you ever gone to the beach and found yourself being "watched" by a piping plover?

PUFFIN

Puffins are seabirds that catch fish by diving down into the water. They usually live in large colonies in cliffs, and they nest in rock crevices or burrowed in the ground. Puffins are recognizable for their black-and-white bodies with bright orange beaks and legs.

Puffins stick together. Sometimes when a puffin couple forms, they find each other at the breeding ground year after year, even 20 years on!

SANDPIPER

Sandpipers are small birds that usually live in groups. They're normally found on beaches, where they use their long beaks to peck at the sand for crustaceans. They're usually a sandy brown color, and they will sometimes wade into the water.

Spotted sandpipers, common on American shores, have interesting gender roles. Male birds are the ones who incubate—keep warm by sitting on—the eggs, and females can have nests of eggs with up to four male partners at a time!

SPOONBILL

A spoonbill always has a utensil at the ready. It wades through shallow water and uses its bill to scoop up prey like a spoon. As it walks, it keeps its mouth open and skims it across the water. As soon as it catches an animal in its mouth, it snaps its bill shut and spoons its prey up.

The pink feathers of the roseate spoonbill, the only spoonbill native to North America, get their color from the birds' diet. Shrimp and crabs eat algae containing carotenoids—yellow, orange, or red pigments—and spoonbills eat shrimp and crabs. The more of these a spoonbill eats, the pinker its feathers will be!

MARINE MAMMALS

Some of the most interesting animals in the ocean are marine mammals. These animals breathe air, but they rely on the ocean to keep them alive. Many marine mammals spend their whole lives in the water, and others live on coasts so that the sea is always close by. Mammals (like humans!) make milk to feed their young, and they are warm-blooded, which means they keep their body warmer than the environment around them. They often have fur, hair, or layers of fat to help keep them warm. This is especially important in the cold ocean in polar regions. Here are a few of the marine mammals that complete the ocean food chain.

DOLPHIN

Dolphins love to play, and they interact with humans all the time. They enjoying playing in the waves made by boats and jumping up above the surface of the water. Spinner dolphins are amazing jumpers—they can leap above the water's surface and spin around up to seven times in the air before they land in the water. Dolphins have a fin on their back called a dorsal fin, and when they're just below the surface with the dorsal fin sticking out it can be easy to confuse them for a shark. The dorsal fin helps them to stay upright and stable in the water. Bottlenose dolphins are one of the most common types, and they're named for their rounded snout.

Dolphins can be pretty noisy. They make a lot of sounds, like whistles and clicks. Whistles help them to communicate with other dolphins. The clicks help them with a special ability called echolocation. They make the clicking noises to send out sound waves. Then they use special organs to sense where the sound waves meet another animal. The sound waves bounce back (echo) to the dolphin, and the information helps them to navigate and hunt.

MANATEE

You'll sometimes hear manatees fondly called sea cows. They're not related to cows at all. They're actually much more closely related to elephants, but they got the nickname because they graze like a cow. Manatees are herbivores, and they graze on plants and seaweed, sometimes eating up to 100 pounds (45.4 kilograms) a day! These slow-moving creatures are very curious, and they are often found in bays. Manatees prefer warm water. They spends half the day sleeping in shallow water, but this can be a pretty risky spot for a nap. Unfortunately, manatees are often hit by passing boats.

Manatees take care of their young for a long time, like humans. The gestation period—time spent in the womb—for a manatee calf is about a year. Then, the mother manatee nurses the calf for up to two years. Part of the bonding process includes the mother manatee and her calf talking to each other. The mother shows her calf where to get food, where to find the warm springs during winter, and which travel routes are best. Manatees don't have very many calves, which means that steps that we humans take to protect them are that much more important!

PORPOISE

Porpoises look a little like dolphins, but there are a few differences between the two. Their teeth and snouts are the easiest way to tell them apart. Many dolphins have long snouts, and they have cone-shaped (conical) teeth. Porpoises usually have smaller mouths, and their teeth are shaped like spades, not cones. They use those flattened teeth to eat all kinds of fish. Because they're mammals, porpoises breathe air. When they need to breathe, they come up to the surface of the water for fresh air. They also have a blowhole. Blowholes allow some marine mammals (like whales, dolphins, and porpoises) to send old air out of their body. Their air spouts out of the blowhole, and then the porpoise takes a new breath of fresh air.

HARBOR PORPOISES

Harbor porpoises—the most common kind—burn a lot of calories throughout the day. That means they need to eat a lot of calories, too. They eat up to 10 percent of their bodyweight in fish per day. Their favorite foods are schooling fish like cod and herring, and they consider octopuses and squids snacks.

ORCA

The orca is sometimes called the killer whale, but this apex predator is technically a member of the dolphin family. That being said, they're a lot bigger than other dolphins, and some orcas have grown up to 25 feet (7.6 meters) long. Orcas are easy to recognize because of their coloring. They have black markings on top of their body, but a white body. This coloring is camouflage. From above, they blend into the darker ocean below them. But from below, they match the lighter color of the sunlit water above them. Many animals never see the orca coming. They live all over the world, and they hunt just about any prey, including fish, sea turtles, birds, and other marine mammals. Orcas often hunt in packs (groups of orcas living together are called pods), and they're smart and effective hunters. They can swim up to 35 miles (56.3 kilometers) per hour, and they use their tails to slap prey so that it's stunned. Even being on shore doesn't keep animals safe from orcas. Hunting groups have been seen using their tails to make waves that hit the shore and knock their prey in the water.

SPYHOPPING

Orcas have an unusual behavior called *spyhopping*, where they pop their upper bodies straight out of the water to look around for prey.

ALL IN THE FAMILY

Orcas are the only mammals known to live with their mothers for their entire lives. And that's quite a long time, since orcas in the wild can live to be 90 years old! Their pods are often family groups descended from one female, and they work together to care for the young orcas.

KILLER WHALE OR HUNTER?

Orcas are sometimes called killer whales, but, in fact, they don't attack humans in the wild. They're excellent hunters, though, and different varieties of orca across the oceans prey on everything from fish to seals to other kinds of whales.

There are about 26,000 wild polar bears in the world today. Something they all have in common is that they like sleep! Polar bears sleep like humans, in one 7- to 8-hour span every day. And if a snowstorm's coming, no problem—polar bears roll over, let the snow blanket over them, and sleep right through it!

COZY CUBS

Baby polar bears are born in dens in the snow, which mother polar bears dig in order to rest safely through the winter. The cubs are usually born in pairs, and their mother keeps them inside for months after they're born, feeding them her milk while she herself loses much of her body weight. When spring comes, mother and cubs leave the den and go in search of food. The cubs will stay with their mother for two years, learning all about how to hunt and survive on the ice.

POLAR BEAR

Bears might not be your first thought when you picture ocean animals, but polar bears are super important to the food chain in polar oceans. Polar bears spend most of their lives on sea ice in the Arctic, and they're great swimmers. Their huge paws help them to paddle, and their fur keeps them warm in the cold water. Polar bears are the biggest bears on the planet, and they can weigh in at over 1,700 pounds (770 kilograms). Their favorite food is seal, and they're super skilled at hunting them. They have strong eyesight (as good as a human's) and a great sense of smell, which means that they can see seals from far away and sniff them out when they're hiding in dens. At the top of the food chain, there are no predators that can take on a polar bear, but that doesn't make them completely safe. The biggest threat to polar bears is climate change (see page 138). Without Arctic ice, it's much harder for them to find food.

SEA LION

Sea lions are often found in cold water, where a layer of fat on their body called blubber helps to keep them warm. They paddle around using their four flippers, and when they're on land sea lions can hold themselves up with their front two flippers. Sea lions look a lot like seals, but the easiest way to tell the difference between the two is by looking at the ears. Sea lions have visible ears, but seals just have an ear hole. Sea lions can grow to be very large. One species, Stellar's sea lion, can grow to be 11 feet (3.4 meters) long and weigh up to 2,500 pounds (1,134 kilograms). Sea lions eat fish and invertebrates, and they're often seen in big groups on rocky beaches.

During mating season, male sea lions, called bulls, can be rude to each other. They set up territories on a rocky coastline, where they welcome female sea lions, but if other male sea lions show up and get too close, they stare, bark, roar, and lunge to get the message—Go away!—across.

SEA OTTER

Sea otters are some of the smallest marine mammals in the ocean. They're a part of the weasel family, and they usually only grow to be about 4 feet (1.2 meters) long. Unlike whales or sea lions with blubber to keep them warm, sea otters stay cozy in the ocean thanks to a thick layer of brown fur. Sea otters are known for being very playful, and one of their favorite foods is the purple sea urchin found in kelp forests (see page 44).

Sea otters' skin has up to a million hair follicles per square inch—the thickest fur of any mammal on earth! How many hair follicles do you have per square inch?

SEAL

Seals are excellent swimmers that can stay under the water for hours, and they can be fierce hunters. Leopard seals are especially well-known for preying on penguins. And although seals are high up on the food chain, they're not always at the top. Polar bears love to eat seals, especially ringed seals in the Arctic. Seals have four webbed flippers that are much better for swimming than they are for being on land. Unlike sea lions, seals can't use their front flippers to hold themselves up.

WEDDELL SEAL

RINGED SEAL